Leicester Ambrose Sawyer

The Bible

Analyzed, translated and accompanied with critical Studies

Leicester Ambrose Sawyer

The Bible
Analyzed, translated and accompanied with critical Studies

ISBN/EAN: 9783337171551

Printed in Europe, USA, Canada, Australia, Japan

Cover: Foto ©ninafisch / pixelio.de

More available books at **www.hansebooks.com**

THE BIBLE:

ANALYZED, TRANSLATED AND ACCOMPANIED WITH

CRITICAL STUDIES,

PUBLISHED IN PARTS OF BOOKS, SINGLE BOOKS AND COLLECTIONS
OF BOOKS, BY

REV. LEICESTER A. SAWYER.

ABRAHAM. GEN. 12: 1—25: 11.

WHITESBORO, N. Y.
L. A. SAWYER.
1884.

T. J. GRIFFITHS, PRINTER, UTICA.

CONTENTS.

I. ABRAHAM.

ANALYSIS—1, Abraham, 100 years; 2, Isaac, 105 years; 3, Jacob, 27 years; 4, Levi, 56 years; 5, Kohath, 71 years; Amram, 71 years; total, 430 years.

1. ABRAHAM, 100 YEARS.

CHAPTER I. 12: 1—20.

Covenants I. and II.; Abram goes with Lot to Palestine, thence to Egypt, has trouble about his wife and returns to Palestine.

12: 1. Jeve said to Abram: Go out from your land, and kindred, and from your father's house, to the land that I will show you;

2. And I will make you a great nation and bless you, and make your name great, and it shall be a blessing;

3. And I will bless him that blesses you, and curse him that curses you; and in you shall all the families of the earth be blessed.

4. And Abram went as Jeve commanded him, and Lot went with him.

5. And Abram was 75 years old when he went from Haran;

6. And he took Sari his wife, and Lot his brother's son, and all their goods they had acquired and the souls [slaves] they had gained in Haran, and went to go to Palestine ; and they came to Palestine.

7. And Abram passed through it to the place of Shechem, to the oak of the teacher, and the Canaanite was then in the land.

8. And Jeve appeared to Abram and said, I will give this land to your seed ; and he built an altar for Jeve that appeared to him.

9. And he removed from there to a mountain east of Bethel, and pitched a tent, with Bethel on the west, and Ai on the east, and he built there an altar for Jeve, and called on the name of Jeve.

9. And Abram went further south.

10. And there was a famine in the land, and he went down to Egypt to sojourn there, for the famine was severe in the land.

11. And it came to pass when he was about to enter Egypt, that he said to Sari his wife: Behold now, I know that you are a woman of fair appearance,

12. And it will come to pass, when the Egyptians see you, that they will say : This is his wife : and they will kill me, and save you alive ;

13. Say, I pray you, that you are my sister, that it may be well with me, because of you, that my life may be spared.

14. And it came to pass when Abram went to Egypt, that the Egyptians saw the woman, that she was very fair.

15. And Pharoe's princes saw her and praised he r

to Pharoe; and the woman was taken to Pharoe's house.

16. And it was well with Abram because of her; and he had sheep, cattle, asses, men servants, women servants, she asses and camels.

17. And Jeve smote Pharoe and his house with great plagues, because of Sari, Abram's wife.

18. And Pharoe called Abram and said: What is this that you did to me? Why did you not tell me that she was your wife?'

19. Why did you say: She is my sister, that I might take her to me for a wife? and now behold your wife, take her and go.

20. And Pharoe commanded men concerning him and sent him away, and his wife, and all that he had.

CHAPTER II. 13: 1—18.

Abram returns to Palestine; he is left by Lot and receives covenant III. 13: 1—18.

13: 1. And Abram went up from Egypt with his wife and all that he had ‹ and Lot went with him, to the south [of Palestine.]

2. And Abram was very rich in cattle, silver and gold.

3. And he went in his removals from the south to Bethel, the place where his tent was at first, between Bethel and Ai,

4. To the place of the altar that he made there at first, and there Abram called on the name of Jeve.

5. And Lot also, who went with Abram, had flocks, herds and tents.

6. And the land could not bear them to live together, for their wealth was great, and they could not live together.

7. And there was strife between the herdmen of Abram and the herdmen of Lot; and the Canaanite and Perizzite then dwelt in the land.

8. And Abram said to Lot: Let there be no strife, I pray you, between me and you, nor between my herdmen and your herdmen, for we are brothers.

9. Is not all the land before you? Separate yourself now from me; if you go to the left, I will go to the right; and if you go to the right, I will go to the left.

10. And Lot lifted up his eyes, and saw all the tract of the Jordan, that it was well watered before Jeve destroyed Sodom and Gomore, like a garden of Jeve, like the land of Egypt, as you go to Zur [Zoar.]

11. And Lot chose the tract of the Jordan, and moved east, and they separated from each other.

12. And Abram dwelt in Palestine, and Lot in the tract [of the Jordan], and pitched his tent in Sodom.

13. And the men of Sodom were wicked and sinned greatly against Jeve.

14. Jeve said to Abram after Lot separated from him: Lift up your eyes now and see from the place where you are, north, south, east and west,

15. For all the land which you see will I give you and your seed forever.

16. And I will make your seed like the dusts of the

earth. If a man can number the dusts of the earth,
then shall your seed be numbered.

17. Rise and go about the land, through its length
and breadth ; for I will give it to you.

18. And Abram moved his tent and went and dwelt
in the oaks of Mamra, which were in Hebron, and
built an altar to Jeve.

CHAPTER III. 14: 1—29.

Abram fights successfully, and is blessed by Melchisedec.

14: 1. And it came to pass in the days of Amraphal king of Shinar, Arioch king of Allasar, Kedorlumer king of Elam, and Tidal king of Goim,

2. That they made war on Bera king of Sodom,
Birsha king of Gomore, Senab king of Adme, Shem-
abar king of Zeboim, and the king of Bela, which is
Zur.

3. All these kings formed an alliance in the vale of
Siddim, which was by the salt sea.

4. Twelve years they served Kedorlumer ; in the
thirteenth year they rebelled :

5. And in the fourteenth year came Kedorlumer
and the kings with him, and smote the Rephaim in
Ashteroth Karnim, the Zuzim in Ham, the Emim in
the plain of Kerithim,

6. And the Horites in their mount Seir, even to
Ail Paran, which was before the wilderness.

7. And they returned and came to Ain Mishpat,
which was Kadesh, and smote all the country of the
Amalekites, and also the Amorites who dwelt in Haz-
zon-tamar.

8. And the kings of Sodom, Gomore, Zeboim and Bela, which is Zur, went out and set themselves in battle array in the vale of Siddim,

9. Against Kedorlumer king of Elam, Tidal king of Goim, Amraphal king of Shinar, and Arioch king of Ellasar, four kings against five.

10. And the vale of Siddim was full of pits of bitumen; and the kings of Sodom and Gomore fled and fell there, and the rest fled to the mountain.

11. And they took all the goods of Sodom and Gomore, and all their provisions, and went away;

12. And they took Lot, Abram's brother, and his goods; for he dwelt in Sodom.

13. And one that escaped, came and told Abram the Hebrew; and he dwelt in the oaks of Mamra the Amorite, brother of Ashcol and Aner, who were in covenant with him.

14. When Abram heard that his brother was taken captive, he led out his trained men, those born in his house, three hundred and eighteen, and pursued the enemy to Dan;

15. And he divided his troops that night, and his servants smote them, and pursued them to Hobe, west of Damascus.

16. And he recovered all the goods, and brought back Lot and his goods, and the women, and the people.

17. And the king of Sodom went out to meet him after his return from smiting Kedorlumer, and the kings that were with him, to the valley of Sheve, which is the king's vale [Hezekiah's.]

18. And Melchisedec king of Salem, brought out

bread and wine; and he was a priest of Al Olion, [the god Olion.]

19. And he blessed him and said: Blessed be Abram of Al Olion, possessor of heaven and earth,

20. And blessed be Al Olion, who gave your enemies into your hand; and he gave him a tenth of all.

21. And the king of Sodom said to Abram, Give me the souls, and take the goods for yourself.

22. And Abram said to the king of Sodom, I lifted my hand to Jeve Al Olion, possessor of heaven and earth,

23. That I will not take a thing that is yours, from a thread to a shoe-string, lest you should say, I made Abram rich ;

24. Except only what the young men ate, and the portion of the men that went with me, Aner, Ashcol and Mamra ; let them take their portions.

CHAPTER IV. 15: 1—20.

Abram receives covenant IV., sealed with sacrifices.

15: 1. After these things came the Word of Jeve in a vision, saying : Fear not, Abram ; I am your shield, and your very great reward.

2. And Abram said: Master Jeve, what will you give me, when I go childless and the steward of my house is this Eleazar of Damascus ?

3. And Abram said : Behold, you have given me no seed ; and behold, a son of my house will be my heir.

4. And behold, the Word of Jeve came to him say-

ing: This [man] shall not be your heir; but one to come from your loins shall be your heir.

5. And he led him out and said: Look now at the heavens and count the stars if you can; and he said to him, So shall your seed be.

6. And he believed Jeve, and he counted it to him for righteousness.

7. And he said to him, I am Jeve, who brought you from Ur of the Chaldeans, to give you this land for a possession.

8. And he said, Master Jeve, how shall I know that I shall possess it?

9. And he said to him: Take for me a heifer and ram, each three years old, a turtle dove, and a young pigeon;

10. And he took all these, and divided them in the middle, and put one part against another, but divided not the birds.

11. And birds of prey came down on the carcasses, and Abram drove them away.

12. And when the sun set, a deep sleep fell on Abram, and behold a terror of great darkness fell on him,

13. And Jeve said to Abram, Know surely that your seed shall be a stranger in a land not theirs; and they shall cause them to serve, and afflict them four hundred years.

14. Then I will judge the nation that they shall serve, and afterwards they shall come forth with great riches.

15. But you shall come to your fathers in peace, and be buried in a good old age;

16. And in the fourth generation they shall return hither, for the iniquity of the Amorites is not yet full.

17. And it came to pass when the sun went down that there was darkness; and behold, there was a smoking furnace, and burning lamp, that passed between these pieces.

18. On that day Jeve made a covenant with Abram, saying: I will give this land to your seed, from the river of Egypt to the great river Euphrates ;

19. The Kenites, Kenizites, Cadmonites,

20. Hittites, Perizites, Rephaim,

21. Amorites, Canaanites, Girgashites and Jebusites.

CHAPTER V.   16 : 1—16.

Abram has Ishmael by Hagar; Story of Hagar.

16 : 1. And Sari, Abram's wife, bore him no children, and she had an Egyptian maid-servant, whose name was Hagar.

2. And Sari said to Abram : Behold now, Jeve has restrained me from bearing ; go in, I pray you, to my maid-servant ; perhaps I may be built up from her. And Abram heard to Sari.

3. And Sari, Abram's wife, took Hagar, her Egyptian maid-servant, at the end of ten years of Abram's dwelling in Palestine, and gave her to Abram, her husband, to be his wife.

4. And he went in to Hagar, and she conceived; and when she saw that she had conceived, she despised her mistress.

5. And Sari said to Abram, My wrong be on you ;

I put my maid-servant in your bosom, and when she
saw that she had conceived, she despised me ; let Jeve
judge between me and you.

6. And Abram said to Sari : Behold, your maid-
servant is in your hand ; do to her as seems good in
your sight. And Sari afflicted her, and she fled from
her presence.

7. And angel Jeve found her by a fountain in the
wilderness, by the fountain in the way to Shur,

8. And said : Hagar, Sari's maid-servant, whence
did you come ? and whither are you going ? And she
said, I fled from the presence of my mistress Sari.

9. And angel Jeve said to her : Return to your
mistress, and endure hardship under her hand.

10. And angel Jeve said to her, I will surely multiply greatly your seed, and it shall not be numbered
for multitude.

11. And angel Jeve said to her, Behold, you are
with child, and you shall bear a son, and call him
Ishmael, for Jeve heard of your affliction ;

12. And he shall be a wild man ; his hand shall be
against every man, and every man's hand against him;
and he shall dwell in the presence of all his brothers.

13. And she called on the name of Jeve, who spoke
to her, saying, You are an Al that sees me ; for she
said : Have I not here seen him that looks after me?

14. Therefore they called the well Barlahiri, [well
of him that saw me]. Behold, it is between Kadesh
and Bered.

15. And Hagar bore Abram a son ; and Abram
called him Ishmael.

16. And Abram was 86 years old when Hagar bore Ishmael to him.

CHAPTER VI. 17: 1—27.

Abram receives from Shaddi covenant V., with circumcision.

17: 1. And Abram was 99 years old, and Jeve [a god] appeared and said to him : I am Al Shaddi ; walk before me and be perfect ;

2. And I will make my covenant between me and you, and multiply you exceedingly.

3. And Abram fell on his face, and God spoke to him, saying :

4. Behold, my covenant is with you, and you shall be a father of a multitude of nations.

5. You shall no more be called Ab-ram [high father], but Abraham [father of a multitude] ; for I will make you a father of a multitude of nations.

6. And I will make you exceedingly fruitful, and make nations of you ; and kings shall be born from you.

7. I will establish my covenant between me and you, and your seed after you in their generations, for an eternal covenant, to be a god to you and to your seed after you ;

8. And I will give you and your seed after you, the land of your sojourning, all Palestine, for an eternal possession ; and I will be their God.

9. And God said to Abraham : You shall keep my covenant, you and your seed after you, for their generations.

10. This is the covenant which you shall keep between me and you, and between your seed after you; every male of you shall be circumcised.

11. And you shall circumcise the flesh of your foreskin, and it shall be a sign of the covenant between me and you.

12. A son of eight days shall be circumcised among you, every male of your generations, the child of the house, the purchase of money, and every son of a stranger that is not from your seed, shall be circumcised.

13. The child of your house shall be circumcised, and the purchase of money, and my covenant shall be in your flesh, for an eternal covenant;

14. And the uncircumcised male shall be cut off from his people; he has broken my covenant.

15. And God said to Abraham : Sari, your wife, shall not be called Sari [my princes], but Sarah [princess.]

16. And I will bless her, and give you a son from her; and she shall be [a mother of] nations, and kings of peoples shall be born from her.

17. And Abraham fell on his face and laughed, and said in his heart : Shall a son be born to one a hundred years old ? and shall Sarah bear at the age of ninety years ?

18. And Abraham said to the god : O that Ishmael may live before you !

19. And God said : Sarah your wife shall surely bear you a son, and you shall call him Isaac [Laughter], and I will establish my covenant with him, and with his seed after him, for an eternal covenant.

20. I have heard you also for Ishmael; behold, I will bless and multiply him; I will make him fruitful and multiply him exceedingly; he shall beget twelve princes, and I will make him a great nation.

21. And I will establish my covenant with Isaac, whom Sarah shall bear to you, in due time the next year.

22. And he ceased to speak with Abraham, and God ascended from before him.

23. Then Abraham took Ishmael his son, and all the children of his house, and the purchase of his money, every male among the men of his house, and circumcised the flesh of their foreskin in that same day, as God commanded him.

24. And Abraham was ninety-nine years old,

25. And Ishmael his son, thirteen years old, when he circumcised the flesh of their foreskin;

26. Abraham and Ishmael his son were circumcised on that same day;

27. And all the men of his house, the child of his house, and the purchase of money from a stranger, were circumcised with him.

CHAPTER VII. 18: 1—33.

Jeve and two other celestials entertained; Jeve again promises Abraham a son by Sarah, and tells him of his purpose in respect to Sodom; Abraham intercedes for Sodom.

18: 1. And Jeve appeared to him in the oaks of Mamra, and he was sitting at his tent door in the heat of the day;

2. And he lifted up his eyes and looked, and behold three men stood before him; and he saw, and ran to meet them from the tent door, and bowed himself to the ground,

3. And said, Masters, if now I have found favor in your sight, go not, I pray you, by your servant;

4. Let now a little water be brought, and do you wash your feet, and rest yourselves under the tree.

5. I will bring a mouthful of bread; and do you refresh yourselves, and then you shall pass on; because for this have you come to your servant. And they said : Well, do as you have said.

6. And Abraham hastened to the tent to Sarah, and said : Prepare quickly three seahs [36 quarts] of flour, knead it and make cakes.

7. And Abraham ran to the herd and took a calf tender and good, and gave it to the boy, and he hastened to dress it.

8. And he took butter and milk, and the calf which he had cooked, and set food before them, and stood by them under the tree, and they ate.

9. And they said to him : Where is Sarah your wife? And he said : Behold, in the tent.

10. And [Jeve] said : I will surely return to you at the time for a life [a birth], and behold, Sarah your wife shall have a son. And Sarah heard at the tent door, for he was behind it.

11. And Abraham and Sarah were old, and it had ceased to be with Sarah, in the manner of women;

12. And Sarah laughed within herself, saying, After I have become old, shall I have pleasure still, and my master is old ?

13. And Jeve said : Abraham, why is this ? Sarah laughed, saying : Shall I really bear when I am old ?

14. Is anything too wonderful for Jeve? In due time I will return to you, at the time for a birth, and Sarah shall have a son.

15. And Sarah lied, saying : I did not laugh, for she was afraid. But he said : No, you certainly did laugh.

16. And the men rose up from there and looked toward Sodom ; and Abraham went with them to see them on the way.

17. And Jeve said : Shall I hide this thing which I do from Abraham ?

17. Abraham will surely be a great and strong nation, and all nations of the earth will be blessed in him. ·

19. For I know him, that he will command his sons and his house after him, and they will keep the way of Jeve, to do righteousness and judgment, that Jeve may bring on Abraham all that he has said concerning him.

20. And Jeve said : There is a cry of distress from Sodom and Gomore, for it is great, and of their sin, for it is extremely oppressive ;

21. I will go down now and see if they have done entirely according to her cry that has come to me, and if not I will know.

22. And the men turned from them and went toward Sodom ; but Abraham stood yet before Jeve ;

23. And Abraham came near and said : Will you indeed destroy the righteous with the wicked ?

24. Perhaps there are fifty righteous men in the

city ; will you destroy, and not spare the place for fifty righteous men that are in it ?

25. Far be it from you to do according to this thing ; to kill the righteous with the wicked, and that it should be with the righteous as with the wicked. Will not the judge of all the earth do right?

26. And Jeve said : If I find fifty righteous men in the city, I will spare the whole place for their sake.

27. And Abraham answered and said : Behold now I have taken it on me to speak to my master, though I am dust and ashes,

28. Perhaps there will lack five of the fifty righteous men. Will you for the lack of five destroy all the city ? And he said : I will not destroy [the city] if I find there forty-five.

29. And he spoke to him yet again, and said : Perhaps there will be found 40 ? And he said : I will not destroy [it] for 40.

30. And he said : Let not [my master] be angry, and I will speak [further]. Perhaps there will be found there thirty. And he said : I will not destroy it if I find thirty.

31. And he said : Behold now I have taken it on me to speak to my master, perhaps twenty will be found there. And he said : I will not destroy it for twenty.

32. And he said : Let not [my master] be angry, and I will speak this once : Perhaps ten will be found there. And he said : I will not destroy it for ten.

33. And Jeve went away when he had finished speaking with Abraham ; and Abraham returned to his place.

CHAPTER VIII.   19 : 1—38.

The two angels that left Abraham visit Lot, and are en-tertained by him ; vile conduct of the Sodomites ; the city destroyed ; Lot and two daughters saved, and their subsequent misdoings.

19 : 1. And the two angels came to Sodom at eve-ning ; and Lot sat in the gate of Sodom ; and Lot saw, and rose up to meet them, and bowed his face to the ground.

2. And said : See here, my masters, turn, I pray you, to the house of your servant, and lodge, and wash your feet, and rise early and go on your way. And they said : No, but we will lodge in the street ;

3. But he urged them much, and they went with him ; and he came to his house, and made them a feast, and baked unleavened cakes, and they ate.

4. They had not yet laid down, when the men of the city surrounded the house, young and old, all the people from the extreme [parts of the city].

5. And they called to Lot, and said to him : Where are the men that came to you to-night ? Bring them out that we may know them.

6. And Lot went out of the door to them, and shut the door after him,

7. And said : Do no wrong, brothers.

8. Behold now I have two daughters, who have not known man ; them will I bring out to you, and do to them as is good in your sight ; only to these men do nothing ; for therefore came they under the shadow of my roof.

9. But they said : Stand back ; and they said : This

2

·man came to sojourn, and now he will be a judge ; we will do worse to you than to them ; and they pressed Lot exceedingly, and drew near to break down the door.

10. And the men put out their hands and took Lot in to them ;

11. And smote the men with blindness, from the least to the greatest of them, and they strove in vain to find the door.

12. And the men said to Lot : Whom have you here? your son-in-law, sons and daughters? all whom you have in the city bring out from this place,

13. For their cry is great before Jeve, and he has sent us to destroy it.

14. And Lot went out and spoke to his sons-in-law, who had married his daughters, and said : Rise, and come out of this place, for Jeve will destroy the city ; and he was in the sight of his sons-in-law as one that mocked.

15. And when the morning came, the angels hastened Lot, saying : Rise, take your wife and two daughters, that are found here, lest you be consumed in the iniquity of the city.

16. And while he lingered, the men took his hand, and his wife's hand, and the hands of his two daughters, in the kindness of Jeve for him, and brought him out, and set him down without the city.

17. And it came to pass, when they had brought them out, that they said to them : Escape for your lives, look not behind you, nor stay in all the plain, escape to the mountain, lest you be destroyed.

18. And Lot said to them : No, masters ;

19. Behold now your servant has found favor in your sight, and you have dealt very kindly with me, to save my life; I can not escape to the mountain, lest evil overtake me and I die;

20. Behold now this city is near to flee to, and it is small; let me escape thither; is it not small? and my life will be saved?

21. And he said to him: Behold I have accepted you in this, not to destroy the city of which you speak.

22. Hasten your escape thither, for I can do nothing till you have gone there; therefore he called the name of the place Zur [Zoar].

23. The sun went forth on the earth, and Lot went to Zur.

24. And Jeve rained on Sodom and Gomore brimstone and fire from Jeve out of heaven;

25. And overthrew those cities, and all the plain, and all the inhabitants of the cities, and that which grew on the ground.

26. And his wife looked back from behind him, and became a pillar of salt.

27. And Abraham rose early in the morning, and [went] to the place where he stood before Jeve,

28. And looked towards Sodom and Gomore, and over all the face of the plain, and saw, and behold the smoke of the land went up like the smoke of a furnace.

29. And it came to pass, when God destroyed the cities of the plain, that he remembered Abraham, and sent Lot from the midst of the destruction when he destroyed the cities in which he dwelt.

30. And Lot went up from Zur, and dwelt on a mountain, and his two daughters with him ; for he was afraid to dwell in Zur, and he and his two daughters dwelt in a cave.

31. And the firstborn said to the younger: Our father is an old man, and there is not a man in the land to come in to us after the manner of all the earth ;

32. Come, let us make our father drink wine, and we will lie with him, and preserve seed from our father.

33. And they made their father drink wine that night, and the firstborn came and slept with her father, and he knew not when she lay down nor when she rose.

34. And it came to pass on the next day that the firstborn said to the younger: Behold I lay with my father yesterday, let us make him drink wine to-night also, and do you go and lie with him, that we may save seed from our father.

35. And they made their father drink wine that night also, and the youngest [daughter] rose and lay with him, and he knew not when she lay down, nor when she rose.

36. And the two daughters of Lot conceived by their father,

37. And the firstborn bore a son, and called him Moab. He is the father of Moab to this day. [715 B. C.]

38. And the younger also bore a son, and she called him Ben-ammi ; he is the father of the sons of Ammon to this day.

CHAPTER IX. 20: 1—18.

Abraham goes to Gerar, and has trouble there on account of his wife.

20 : 1. Abraham moved from there south, and dwelt between Kadesh and Shur, and sojourned in Gerar.

2. And Abraham said of Sarah : She is my sister ; and Abimelech, king of Gerar, sent and took Sarah.

3. And God came to Abimelech in a dream by night, and said to him: Behold you are a dead man, because of the woman whom you have taken ; for she is a husband's wife.

4. And Abimelech had not approached her ; and he said : Master, will you destroy a righteous nation ?

5. Said he not to me: She is my sister ? and also said she not: He is my brother ? In the integrity of my heart and in the innocency of my hands I did this.

6. And the god said to him in a dream : I know that in the integrity of your heart you did this, and I held you back from sinning against me. For that reason I did not suffer you to touch her.

7. And now return the man's wife, for he is a prophet, and will pray for you, and you shall live ; but if you do not return her, know that you shall certainly die, and all that belongs to you.

8. Then Abimelech rose early in the morning, and called all his servants, and told all these things in their ears, and the men feared greatly.

9. And Abimelech called Abraham, and said to him : What have you done to us ? and in what did I

sin against you, that you brought on me and on my kingdom this great sin ? You did to me things that · should not be done.

10. And Abimelech said to Abraham : What did you see, that you did this thing ?

11. And Abraham said : I said, Surely there is no fear of gods in this place ; and they will kill me because of my wife.

12. And really also she is my sister ; she is the daughter of my father, but not of my mother, and she became my wife.

13. And it came to pass when gods caused me to wander from my father's house, that I said to her : This is the kindness which you shall do me in every place where we go ; say of me : He is my brother.

14. And Abimelech took sheep, cattle, men servants and maid servants, and gave [them] to Abraham, and restored to him Sarah his wife.

15. And Abimelech said : Behold my land is before you, dwell where you please.

16. And he said to Sarah : Behold I have given your brother a thousand [shekels] of silver [$600] ; behold he shall be to you for a covering of the eyes to all that are with you, and to all. [Thus] was she reproved.

17. And Abraham prayed to the God ; and God healed Abimelech, his wife, and his maid servants, and they bore children ;

18. For Jeve had closed every womb of the house of Abimelech because of Sarah, Abraham's wife.

CHAPTER X. 21 : 1—21.

Isaac is born, and Hagar and Ishmael are banished.

21 : 1. And Jeve visited Sarah, and did to her as he said ;

2. And Sarah conceived, and bore a son to Abraham in his old age, at the set time, as God said to them.

3. And Abraham called his son, whom Sarah bore to him, Isaac.

4. And Abraham circumcised Isaac when he was eight days old, as God commanded him.

5. And Abraham was an hundred years old when Isaac was born to him.

6. And Sarah said : God has made me laugh, and every one that hears will laugh with me.

7. And she said : Who would have told Abraham that Sarah would nurse sons? but I have borne a son to his old age.

8. And the child grew, and was weaned ; and Abraham made a great feast on the day that Isaac was weaned.

9. And Sarah saw the son of Hagar, the Egyptian, which she bore to Abraham, mock ;

10. And she said to Abraham : Cast out this maid servant and her son, for the son of this maid servant shall not inherit with my son Isaac.

11. And the thing was evil in the sight of Abraham, concerning his son.

12. And God said to Abraham : Let it not be evil

in your sight concerning the child, nor concerning
• your maid servant; in all that Sarah says to you, hear
to her, for in Isaac shall your seed be called.

13. And as to the son of the maid servant, I will
make a nation also of him because he is your son.

14. And Abraham rose early in the morning, and
took bread and a leather bottle of water, and gave
them to Hagar, and put them on her shoulder, and
the child, and sent her away, and she went and wan-
dered in the wilderness of Barsheba.

15. And the water was used in the bottle, and she
cast the child under one of the bushes,

16. And went and sat down by herself at the distance of the drawing of a bow, for she said : I can not
see the child die ; and she sat down before [him], and
lifted up her voice and wept.

17. And God heard the voice of the boy ; and the
angel of God called to Hagar out of heaven, and said
to her : What is the matter with you, Hagar? Fear
not; for God heard the voice of the boy where he is.

18. Rise, take the boy, and hold him in your hand,
for I will make of him a great nation.

19. And God opened her eyes, and she saw a well
of water, and went and filled the bottle with water,
and gave the boy drink.

20. And God was with the boy, and he grew, and
dwelt in the wilderness, and was a great archer.

21. And he dwelt in the wilderness of Paran, and
his mother took him a wife from the land of Egypt.

CHAPTER XI. 21 : 22—34.

Abraham makes a covenant with the king of Gerar.

21 : 22. And it came to pass at that time that Abimelech and Phicol, the general of his army, spoke to Abraham, saying : God is with you in all that you do.

23. And now swear to me by God, that you will not deal falsely with me, nor with my son, nor my son's son. According to the kindness which I have shown you, do you deal with me, and with the land in which you have sojourned.

24. And Abraham said : I will swear.

25. And Abraham reproved Abimelech because of a well of water which Abimelech's servants took by force.

26. And Abimelech said : I knew not who did this thing, neither did you tell me, nor did I hear of it till to-day.

27. And Abraham took sheep and cattle and gave them to Abimelech, and they made a covenant.

28. And Abraham set apart seven ewe lambs of the flock ;

29. And Abimelech said : What mean these seven ewe lambs that you have set apart ?

30. And he said : Verily, these seven ewe lambs shall you take from my hand, that it may be for a witness that I dug this well.

31. Therefore he called that place, because they swore there, Barshcba.

32. And Abimelech and Phicol the general of his army rose, and returned to the land of the Philistines.

33. And he planted a grove in Barsheba, and called there on the name of Jeve, the Al eternal.

34. And Abraham sojourned in the land of the Philistines many days.

CHAPTER XII. 22 : 1—19.

God tempts Abraham, and Jeve gives him Covenant VI.

22 : 1. And it came to pass after these things, that the God tempted Abraham ; and he said to him, Abraham : and he said : Behold me.

2. And he said : Take now your dear son, Isaac, whom you love, and go to the land of Moriah, and offer him there for a burnt offering on one of the mountains of which I will tell you.

3. And Abraham rose early in the morning, and harnessed his ass, and took two of his servants with him, and Isaac his son ; and split wood for the sacrifice, and rose and went to the place of which the God told him.

4. On the third day he lifted up his eyes, and saw the place afar off.

5. And Abraham said to his servants : Stay here with the ass, and I and the boy will go yonder and worship, and return to you.

6. And Abraham took the wood for the burnt offering, and put it on Isaac his son, and took in his hand the fire and the knife ; and the two went together.

7. And Isaac spoke to Abraham his father, and said : Behold the fire and the wood, and where is the sheep for a burnt offering ?

8. And Abraham said, God will provide him the sheep for a burnt offering, my son. And the two went on together.

9. And they came to the place of which the God told him. And Abraham built there an altar, and arranged the wood, and bound Isaac his son, and laid him on the altar on the wood.

10. And Abraham stretched forth his hand, and took the knife to kill his son.

11. And angel Jeve called to him from heaven, and said : Abraham, Abraham, and he said : Behold me.

12. And he said : Lay not your hand on the boy, nor do a thing to him. For now I know that you fear gods, since you withheld not your beloved son from me.

13. And Abraham lifted up his eyes and saw and behold a ram was behind him caught in a thicket by his horns; and Abraham went and took the ram, and offered him for a burnt offering instead of his son.

14. And Abraham called the place Jeve-jire [Jeve will provide], and it is said to [this] day, Jeve will provide on the mountain.

15. And angel Jeve called to Abraham a second time from heaven,

16. And said to him, I swore by myself, says Jeve, because you did this, and withheld not your son, your much-loved son,

17. That I will surely bless you, and multiply your seed as the stars of heaven, and as the sands on the sea shore ; your seed shall possess the gate of his enemies,

18. And in your seed shall all the nations of the earth be blessed, because you obeyed my voice.

19. And Abraham returned to his servants, and they arose and went together to Barsheba.

CHAPTER XIII. 22: 20—24.

The family of Nahor. 22: 20—24.

22: 20. And it came to pass after these things, that it was told Abraham, saying: Behold, Milke also has borne sons to your brother Nahor,

21. Uz his first born, Buz his brother, Kemual father of Aram [Syria],

22. Chesed, Hazo, Pildash, Idlaph and Bethuel.

23. And Bethuel begat Rebecca. Milke bore these eight to Nahor, Abraham's brother.

24. And his concubine, whose name was Reume, also bore him Tebah, Gaham, Tahash and Moche.

CHAPTER XIV.

Sarah dies, and Abraham buys a field for a burying place. 23: 1—20.

23: 1. And the life of Sarah was one hundred and twenty-seven years.

2. And Sarah died in Kirith-arba, which is Hebron in Palestine. And Abraham came to lament for Sarah and to mourn for her;

3. And Abraham arose from before his dead, and spoke to the sons of Heth, saying:

4. I am a stranger and sojourner with you; give

me a possession of a burying place with you, that I may bury my dead from my sight.

5. And the sons of Heth answered Abraham, saying to him :

6. Hear me, master, you are a prince of God among us ; in the choice of our burying places, bury your dead; not a man of us will hinder you from burying your dead.

7. And Abraham rose and bowed to the people of the land, the sons of Heth,

8. And spoke to them, saying: If it is your mind that I should bury my dead from my sight, hear me, and entreat for me, Ephron son of Zohar,

9. To give me the cave of Machpele, which belongs to him, which is at the end of his field; it shall be given me for its full value in silver, for a possession, for a burying place.

10. And Ephron, the Hittite, answered Abraham in the hearing of the sons of Heth, of all that enter into the gate of the city, saying :

11. No, my master, hear me ; I give you the field, and the cave which is in it I give you, in the sight of the sons of my people I give it to you ; bury your dead.

12. Then Abraham bowed himself before the people of the land,

13. And spoke to Ephron in the hearing of the people of the land, saying : If you will indeed give it to me, I will will give silver for the field ; take it of me, and I will bury my dead there.

14. And Ephron answered Abraham, saying :

15. My master, hear me ; the land is worth four

hundred shekels of silver ; what is that between you and me? bury your dead.

16. And Abraham heard to Ephron, and weighed to him the silver that he named in the hearing of the sons of Heth, four hundred shekels of silver, current with the merchant, [$240.]

17. And the field of Ephron which was in Machpele, before Mamre, the field and the cave in it, and all the trees in the field, [and] in its borders round about,

18. Were conveyed to Abraham for a possession in the sight of the sons of Heth, of all that enter the gate of the city.

19. And after that, Abraham buried Sarah his wife in the cave of the field of Machpele, before Mamra, which is Hebron in Palestine.

20. And the field and the cave in it, were conveyed to Abraham for a possession for a burying place from the sons of Heth.

CHAPTER XV.   24: 1—57.

Abraham obtains a wife for Isaac from Syria.

24: 1. And Abraham was an old man and advanced in years, and Jeve had blessed him in all things.

2. And Abraham said to his servant, the elder of his house, the ruler of all he had, Put your hand now under my thigh,

3. And I will swear you by Jeve, God of the heavens and God of the earth, that you will not take a wife for my son from the daughters of the Canaanites, among whom I dwell ;

4. But will go to the land of my nativity, and take a wife for my son Isaac.

5. And the servant said to him : Perhaps the woman will not come after me to this land ; shall I take back your son to the land from which you came ?

6. And Abraham said to him : Take heed to yourself that you do not take my son back there.

7. Jeve, God of the heavens, who took me from the home of my father, and from the land of my nativity, and who spoke to me and swore to me, saying : To your seed will I give this land, will send his angel before you, and you shall take a wife for my son from there.

8. And if the woman will not come after you, you shall be released from this my oath ; only take my son back there.

9. And the servant put his hand under Abraham his master's thigh, and was sworn according to this word.

10. And the servant took ten of his master's camels, and went ; all the goods of his master were in his hand ; and he rose and went to Syria, to the city of Nahor.

11. And he caused the camels to kneel at a well outside of the city, at evening, at the time of the coming of the water-carriers,

12. And said : Jeve, God of my master Abraham, prosper me, I pray you, this day, and show kindness to my master.

13. Behold, I will stand by the well, and the daughters of the men of the city will come out to draw water,

14. And let it be that the young woman to whom I shall say : Set down your pail, I pray you, that I may drink ; and she shall say, I will give your camels drink also ; let her be the one whom you have chosen for your servant Isaac ; and by this let me know that you have shown kindness to my master.

15. And it came to pass before he had finished speaking, that, behold, Rebecca came out who was born to Bethuel, son of Milke, wife of Nahor, Abraham's brother, and her pail was on her shoulder.

16. And the girl was of very fair appearance, a virgin, and man had not known her ; and she went down to the fountain, and filled her pail and came up.

17. And the servant ran to meet her, and said : Give me, I pray you, a little water to drink from your pail.

18. And she said : Drink, my master ; and she hastened and let down her pail on her hand, and gave him drink.

19. When she finished giving him drink, she said : I will also draw for the camels, till they have all drunk.

20. And she hastened and emptied her pail into the watering trough, and ran again to the well to draw, and drew for all his camels.

21. And the man wondered at her, and considered, to know whether Jeve had prospered his way or not ;

22. And it came to pass, when the camels had finished drinking, that he took a nose jewel of a half shekel's weight [137 grains] of gold, and two gold bracelets for her hands ;

23. And said : Whose daughter are you? Tell me,

I pray you; is there a place to lodge in your father's house?

24. And she said to him, I am a daughter of Bethuel, son of Milke, whom she bore to Nahor.

25. And she said to him : Both straw and fodder are plenty with us, and there is also a place to lodge.

26. And the man bowed and worshiped Jeve,

27. And said: Blessed be Jeve, god of my master Abraham, who has not left off his kindness, nor his truth from being with my master; I was on the way and he led me to the house of [my master's brother.]

28. And the girl ran and told the house of her mother, according to these words.

29. And Rebecca had a brother, whose name was Laban, and Laban ran out to the man at the well.

30. And when he saw the nose jewel and the bracelets on the hands of his sister, and [heard] the words of Rebecca, saying : Thus said the man to me, he went to the man, and behold, he stood by the camels at the well.

31. And he said : Come, blessed of Jeve, why do you stand without ? I have prepared the house and a place for the camels.

32. And the man came to the house and ungirded the camels; and he gave straw and fodder for the camels, and water to wash his feet, and the feet of the men with him.

33. And food was set before him to eat ; but he said : I will not eat till I tell my business. And he said, Tell.

34. And he said : I am Abraham's servant.

35. And Jeve has blessed my master greatly, and
3

made him great, and given him sheep, cattle, silver,
gold, men servants, maid servants, camels, and asses.

36. And Sarah my master's wife, bore a son to my
master after she had become old, and he has given him
all that he had.

37. And my master swore me, saying: Take not a
wife for my son from the daughters of the Canaanites,
in whose land I dwell;

38. But go to the house of my father and to my
family, and take a wife for my son.

39. And I said to my master: Perhaps the woman
will not come after me.

40. And he said to me: Jeve, before whom I have
walked, will send his angel with you, and prosper
your way, and you shall take a wife for my son from
my family, and from the house of my father.

41. Then you shall be clear from my oath, when
you have gone to my family, if they do not give you.

42. Then I came this day to the well and said:
Jeve, god of my master Abraham, if it is now your
purpose to prosper my way which I have come,

43. Behold I will stand at the well, and it shall be,
that the young woman who shall come to draw water,
and I say to her, Give me, I pray you, a little water
to drink from your pail,

44. And she shall say to me, Drink, and I will also
draw water for the camels; let this be the woman
whom Jeve has chosen for my master's son,

45. And before I had finished speaking in my heart,
behold, Rebecca came out with her pail on her shoulder,
and went down to the well and drew; and I said to
her: Give me, I pray you, a drink.

46. And she hastened and let down her pail from her shoulder, and said : Drink, and I will water the camels also ; and I drank, and she gave the camels drink.

47. Then I asked her, and said : Whose daughter are you? And she said, I am a daughter of Bethuel, son of Nahor, whom Milke bore; and I put the nose jewel on her nose, and the bracelets on her hands,

48. And I bowed and worshiped Jeve, and blessed Jeve, god of my master Abraham, who led me by the way in truth, to take the daughter of my master's brother for his son.

49. And now if you see your way to deal kindly and truly with my master, tell me; and if not, tell me, that I may turn to the right hand or to the left.

50. And Laban and Bethuel answered and said : The thing proceeds from Jeve; we cannot say to you evil or good;

51. Behold, Rebecca is before you ; take her and go, and let her be the wife of your master's son, as Jeve has said.

52. And it came to pass when Abraham's servant heard their words, he bowed himself to the earth to Jeve.

53. And the servant brought out jewels of silver and jewels of gold, and clothes, and gave them to Rebecca, and gave precious things to her brothers, and her mother.   •

54. And they ate and drank, and the men that were with him ; and they lodged, and rose in the morning. Then he said : Send me away to my master.

55. And her brother and mother said : Let the girl

stay with us some days, perhaps ten ; after that she
shall go.

56. But he said to them : Hinder me not, since Jeve
has prospered my way, that I may go to my master.

57. And they said : Let us call the girl and ask her .

58. And they called Rebecca and said to her : Will
you go with this man ?   And she said, I will.

59. And they sent away Rebecca their sister, and
her nurse, and Abraham's servant and his men.

60. And they blessed Rebecca, and said to her : You
are our sister ; may you be thousands and tens of thousands, and may your seed possess the gate of his enemies.

61. And Rebecca rose, and her maidens, and rode
on the camels, and went after the man.   And Isaac's
servant took Rebecca and went.

62. And Isaac went from the entrance of Barlahi-
rai, and dwelt at the south.

63. And he went out to meditate in the field, at the
approach of evening, and lifted up his eyes and looked,
and behold the camels were coming.

64. And Rebecca lifted up her eyes, and saw Isaac,
and she came down from the camel,

65. And said to the servant: Who is that man that
is walking in the field to meet us ?   And the servant
said : That is my master.   And she took a vail and
covered herself.

66. And the servant told Isaac all that he had done.

67. And Isaac brought her to his mother Sarah's
tent ; and he took Rebecca, and she became his wife,
and he loved her ; and Isaac was comforted for his
mother.

CHAPTER XVI.   25: 1—11.

*Abraham marries Keture, has six sons by her, whom he
provides for, and dies.   25: 1—11.*

25 : 1. And Abraham again took a wife, and her
name was Keture.

2. And she bore him Zimran, Ikshan, Midan,
Midin, [Midian], Ishbak and Shuah.

3. And Ikshan begat Sheba and Dedan, and the
sons of Dedan were Assyrians, Letushim and Lammim.

4. And the sons of Midin [Midian], Epher, Sepher,
Enoch, Abida and Aldea.   All of these were sons of
Keture.

5. And Abraham gave all that he had to Isaac ;

6. And to the sons of his concubines he gave gifts,
and sent them east, from before Isaac his son, in his
life time.

7. The life of Abraham was one hundred and seventy-five years ;

8. And Abraham died in a good old age, an old
man full [of years], and was gathered to his people.

9. Isaac and Ishmael, his sons, buried him in the
cave of Macpele, in the field of Ephron son of Zohar
the Hittite, that was before Mamra,

10. The field which Abraham bought of the sons of
Heth.   Abraham and Sarah were buried there.

CRITICAL STUDIES OF THE HEBREW PATRIARCHS. GEN. 12:1—EX. 4:31.

I. *Character of the Work.*

The Bible begins with the book of generations, which constitutes its first eleven chapters ; then follows the book of the patriarchs from Gen. 12 : 1 to 49 : 33, where the author left it incomplete, probably arrested by death. It should have had accounts of Levi, Kohath and Amram, completed after the same method as those of Abraham, Isaac and Jacob, and should have given us many particulars of their times. Instead of this, we have the extravagant account of Jacob's funeral, indidicating a different hand, with different ideas from the author of the preceding, and the first four chapters of Exodus, introducing Moses and the theocracy in the style of the previous Jeve documents.

The books of generations and the patriarchs both describe the prehistoric times of the Hebrews, closing with definite epochs—the book of generations with the death of Terah in Syria, and that of the patriarchs, with the founding of the theocracy by Moses in Egypt, as related in the law of Hezekiah, in 715 B. C. The author of the book of generations makes its time 2,080 years, beginning with creation. The author of the book of the patriarchs gives us 100 years for the patriarchate of Abraham, 105 for that of Isaac,

10 years for that of Jacob in Palestine, and 17 years for that of Jacob in Egypt, and dies after relating the death of Jacob, completing a period of 232 years. The author of the next book, in Ex. 12 : 40, reports the Egyptian period, without defining it, at 430 years. This would naturally require to be reckoned from the descent of Jacob to that country, which would make the entire period from Abraham 75, to Moses 80, 662 years. Josephus, however, in A. J., 2, 15, 2, led the way in making the 430 years of Ex. 12 : 40 take us back to the migration of Abram, and Christian interpreters have followed him in this. The author of the account of the exode appears to have meant, as he says, to give Isral 430 years in Egypt, without saying any thing of his residence elsewhere. How little the Hebrews pretended to know of their generation and patriarchal periods, appears from those books, and how little their actual information was, also appears.

The book of the Patriarchs is a work of genius, and purports to be a history of the Hebrews from the time of their leaving Syria for homes farther south and west, to the founding of the theocracy of Jeve by Moses in Egypt in 1640 B. C. It reports those times neither fully nor correctly. Its stories are chiefly fictions, written under the Davidic kings, with no attestation as narratives of facts ; the writers do not give us their names, ages, conditions, the sources of their information nor their authorities. The just presumption, in view of all these facts, is, that they had no reliable authorities for much which they relate, but that going back from 600 to more than 1600 years, they give us the little that was known of that remote period by the Hebrews in their times, and supplement it with large additions from their imaginations. This clearly appears from the work, which is mainly one of imagination.

It would be no greater blunder to interpret Paradise Lost as a history of the rebellious celestials, their mad misdoings in the earth and the under-world, and the punishments inflicted on them, than it is to interpret the accounts of the Hebrew patriarchs as strictly historic and veritable.

But the general consent of Christendom for 1800 years to receive these accounts as relating only facts, though begun in great ignorance, their acceptance as such by nearly all the colleges and universities, and by church authorities generally, Catholic and Protestant, and their general support by the periodical press, religious and secular, furnish a basis for sophisms in their favor so plausible, and of such force, even with educated men, that few can appreciate evidence to the contrary, however clear or conclusive. Most accept the common opinions because they are common, and have been so long and so reputably accepted. If common and reputable faiths were always correct, it would be right to accept these as correct ; but in the higher fields of thought the common mind generally stops short of recondite truths, and faiths are generally to a great extent loose, uncertain and false.

Besides, depending on this argument for faith, is suspicious ; any opinion that is correct, is known to be so by evidence, and the fact that these accounts are not shown to be correct by evidence, implies that there is no evidence to show their correctness; if there was, intelligent inquirers would find it.

It is worse than childish to cherish the false, and refuse to consider evidence by which it is known to be so. But instances of this daily occur. On account of the great difficulty of appreciating evidence of falsehood and delusion where the falsehood is generally affirmed as true, and the delusion is in high credit, we here give a summary of independent proofs of the correctness of our positions in regard to this book, and ask those who lean on the opinions of the many, to examine them singly, and find a fallacy in them, if there is one. If there is none, intelligent inquirers will abandon their cherished sophisms, and another instance will be added to all that have gone before, in which truth, long ignored and decried, and opposed by great dignities and authorities, is finally master of all fields.

It is base and contemptible to impose on the credulity of the ignorant by putting forth false claims in respect to any books to which they look for information, and it is in some degree dishonorable to be imposed upon by any sophistries, however specious.

It is a great misfortune to believe a lie; and much of the misery of the world comes from believing lies. We can neither believe, nor impose them on others, without guilt. Men may applaud such impostors. but God will certainly condemn them.

The Christian religion puts the responsibility of men for believing the truth on its evidence, in the fore front of all its lessons, by making right believing the condition of all possible good, and disbelieving

the right, of all evil. Good and evil are not condi-
tioned on believing this or that, independently of its
evidences, but on believing intelligently and correctly.
All believing without evidence, and in contradiction
of it, is vicious.

1. *The Arithmetical Proof.*

This was first developed in our times by the late
bishop Colenso, of the Church of England, in Natal,
on the eastern coast of Africa. His showing of this
argument surprised the world, and attracted for a
time much attention. It has not been, and can not be
refuted. It may be neglected for a time, in the false
faith that the church can not so long and so greatly
have misjudged the questions involved, but it will yet
command universal assent; and the name of Colenso
will be had in honor, when his detractors will be for-
gotten, or only remembered as contributing their mite
to hinder an advance of knowledge, led by Colenso.

According to Gen. 46 : 27, the house of Jacob that
went down to Egypt and settled there in the time of
Joseph, were seventy souls. Under Moses, 215 years
later, according to Num. 1 : 46, as commonly interpreted, the twelve tribes, exclusive of Levi and his
sons, numbered an army of 603,550 men. Adding
as many for the corresponding women, we have
1,206,100 souls ; and adding as many more for children and the aged and infirm of both sexes, and we
have 1,810,650. Such an increase from seventy families in 215 years, and any thing like it, is impossible.
The numbers are too great, or the time too short for
history, or both the numbers and the time are in fault.

Manetho, reporting on the subject from official records by the Egyptians, estimates the army of the Hebrews, while dominant in Egypt, at 240,000 men, who were trained and drilled in a single encampment. At the time of their leaving Egypt, he says they were more than 240,000, implying that as far as the Egyptian records showed, they might have left Egypt 300,000 strong. If they left with an army of 300,000, the nation must have exceeded 900,000, a number still much too large to have proceeded from seventy families in 215 years.

This will be further evident if we compare the increase from the sons of Jacob and their children in their Egyptian period, with that from Abraham to Jacob at his descent to Egypt. The increase from Abraham in 215 years, was 70 ; at the same rate the increase from this seventy would be 470 ; and if you multiply this by 10, you get only 4,700. Instead of these small numbers, the census of the second month of the second year from the exode, Num. 1, 46, gives us 603,550 from eleven of the twelve tribes, mustered into the army ; and, according to Ex. 12 : 36, the nation marched from Rameses led by about 600,000 foot [soldiers]. Such an increase in 215 years is impossible.

The above argument is based on the interpretation of the 430 years of Ex. 12: 40, as comprehending the 215 years of Abraham, Isaac and Jacob in Palestine. On the more probable supposition, that it excludes them, and is reckoned from the descent of Jacob to Egypt, and his settlement there, the three generations of Levi, Kohath and Amram are required to occupy these 430 years, making an average generation and patriarchate 143⅓ years, and these three generations are required to account for the vast increase by which seventy souls became a nation led by an army of 603,550 men. At the rate of increase from Abram 75, to Jacob 120, we should have Jacob and his sons making seventy souls ; in 430 years they become 490 souls, and in 645 years, 343,000 souls. This is the number to be obtained from the seventy souls of Jacob in 430 years, instead of 215 years. Making every third soul a soldier, the army with which it would leave Egypt would be 104,333⅓.

On both suppositions, the leaving of Egypt by the Hebrews with an army of 603,550 foot-soldiers is an impossibility, showing that the facts are not as said, and that while the accounts in question may correspond to the facts remotely in the manner of enigmas, they cannot describe them historically. As in geometry one showing establishes a proposition, so here and everywhere one proof settles a historic question ; but, as in geometry, many propositions admit of different independent proofs, so it is here ; and we proceed to others.

2. *The Genealogical Proof.*

The period from Abraham 75 to Moses 80, is measured by six patriarchs and six generations. These average in 430 years 71⅔ years each. If we adopt the more correct interpretation, and make the patriarchal period 645 years, its average generations and patriarchates are 107½ years. In both cases our numbers are too great for history. For the shorter pe-

riod of 430 years we should have thirteen generations
and twenty or thirty chiefs, and for the longer period
of 645 years we should have 19⅓ generations, and
thirty or forty chiefs. The work, therefore, is not
historic.

3. *The Theological Proof.*

The book names three gods acknowledged by the
Hebrews: Olion, the most high; Gen. 14: 18, 19;
Shaddi, the national god of the Hebrews; 17: 1; 28:
3; 35: 11; and Jeve, 12: 1, etc., who is at a later
period put above Shaddi, but below Olion; and is
accompanied and served by angels. Shaddi appears
to Abram, and makes an everlasting covenant with
him, to be a god to him and to his seed after him.
This implies that he would not be equally the god of
all men, and that in being his god and the god of his
descendants he was conferring on him and them a
special favor. The true God is alike the God of all
men and all worlds, and is no respecter of persons.

Shaddi incorporates circumcision into his covenant
with Abraham, an institution that could have originated only among savages.

Jeve first gives the Abrahamic covenant in Syria,
and repeats it three times in Palestine, and the word
of Jeve gives it once in Palestine. The word of
Jeve's covenant is confirmed with sacrifices, but circumcision is confined to that of Shaddi. Two different gods should not be reported as giving the same
covenant.

Jeve and two other celestials visit Abraham at Hebron, and dine with him, partaking of an ample feast,

the meat being killed for them and the bread baked
after their arrival. The same evening the two ac-
companying celestials visit Lot in Sodom, and eat a
liberal supper with him. This is not the manner of
God.

After Isaac had grown to be a young man, God
tempts Abraham to kill him and offer him up as a
burnt offering on mount Moriah ; and Jeve only re-
voked the order after Abraham had bound his son,
laid him like a dumb beast on the wood of the altar,
and had raised the knife to kill him.

Jeve knows nothing by omniscience, but judges
from what he hears and sees, and visits places and
persons to find out the facts about them. This is not
the manner of God.

Jeve promises Abraham the country of other people, to be enjoyed by his seed forever, and this promise is emphasized by repetition, but is not fulfilled. It
is not the manner of God to make such promises.

These stories, therefore, are proved to be not historic by their theology. A correct theology has any
number of celestials, but only one God, the supreme
father and sovereign of all nations, races and worlds.
This God is like the light and heat medium, equally
present in all places, and at all times, and can not be
exhibited under limited forms, human or animal. Nor
can God withdraw himself from any of his creatures ;
all live in him.

The human form is as inadequate to represent God
as that of an ox, elephant or eagle. The nearest re-
semblance to him physically, of which we have any
knowledge, is the light and heat medium. God speaks

to men through men, animals and the universal world, but he speaks only as God, not as a man or animal, and uses no animal or human signs of ideas.

A further proof from contemporary history, we reserve for Study III.

2. *The Abrahamic Covenants.*

These occupy a prominent place in the history of the Caucasians, and are among the most extraordinary and successful impositions ever devised. A covenant is a mutual agreement between parties ; the party giving it, is called the party of the first part, and the party receiving it, the party of the second part. Na, tional and household gods were imagined by the ancients often to visit men, and hold conversations with them. The Hebrews never imagined Olion their most high, to pay such visits, or in any way to communicate with them ; hence it is well said in John 1 : 18, God, meaning the most high, none ever saw ; the only begotten son, who is in the bosom of the father, declared [his messages.]

The covenants given to Abraham are mainly promises, first by Shaddi, then by Jeve, as to what they would do for him and his seed.

There are six of them identical in substance, and nearly so in form. The law of Asa in 950 B. C., found only that given by Shaddi, in Gen. 17 : 1—22, and had it renewed to Jacob after his return with his family from Syria to Palestine, in Gen. 35 : 9—15.

The law of Hezekiah in 715 B. C., omitted these, and gave instead of them, four covenants of Jeve with Abraham, the first in Syria, in Gen. 12 : 1; the sec-

ond in Shechem, Gen. 12 : 7; the third at Bethel,
13 : 5—18, and the fourth at Mount Moriah, 22 :
16—18 ; and had these covenants repeated to Jacob
on his way to Syria to escape from his angry brother,
in Gen. 28 : 10—15.

The law of Josiah in 623 B. C., arranged all these
covenants in a single series, interpolating Shaddi's covenant with Abraham, after the third of Jeve, in Gen.
17 : 1—22 ; Shaddi's covenant with Jacob after that
of Jeve with him, in Gen. 35 : 9—16, and confound-
ing the two gods in the story of the first of these covenants by making Jeve, in Gen. 17 : 1, say, I am Al
Shaddi, which he was not.

Ezra in 450 interpolated this series with the visit
and covenant of the word of Jeve, in Gen. 15 : 1—31.
When the covenant of Shaddi appeared in 950 B. C.
under Asa, its promises had been fulfilled up to that
time. As the nation construed its acquisitions, all of
them were gifts of Jeve, the supposed superior of
Shaddi, and nothing appeared to threaten the nation
with its later disasters. From small beginnings it had
grown to be great and powerful. Tyre, Sidon and
Gaza continued to be independent, but were on terms
of friendship with the Hebrews, and other Palestinian
states had been destroyed. When the covenants of
Jeve were made to supersede those of Shaddi, under
Hezekiah, in 715 B. C., the Davidic kings still reigned
at Jerusalem, and a glorious future was expected by
them to continue without end. The then recent fall
of the northern kingdom removed from Judah a dan-
gerous enemy, and was not greatly deplored by that
sister kingdom ; it left more room for them.

But so far from obtaining their country by gift of
Jeve, they obtained it by violence and murder. The
claim that Jeve ordered them to take it by violence
and slaughter, is either false, invented in later times,
or an imposition practiced on the nation at the time,
by its priests and prophets. God never authorizes
men to acquire property by injustice, still less by murder; and the pretence of his doing it is an impious fraud.
The atrocities that attended the conquest of Palestine
by the Hebrews, were heart-rending, and the nation
before its bloody drama was finished, paid in rivers of
its blood for the blood of the Palestinians which it
wickedly shed. So true is the Christian maxim at-
tributed to Jesus : He that takes the sword shall per-
ish by the sword.

The terrible reverses of the Hebrews beginning with
the fall of the northern kingdom in 722 B. C., and
that of Judah in 588 B. C., are among the most amaz-
ing that ever befell a people, and extend over more
than 2000 years.

The pretended promises concerning Palestine have
failed entirely, since the destruction of Jerusalem by
Titus in 70 A. D., and besides this are such as God
could never make. On this ground alone we safely
conclude that he never did make them ; but they are
further shown to be fraudulent by their non-fulfill-
ment. Forged notes from men may sometimes be
honored, but forged covenants for God are sure to
come to grief.

God gives lands and other property by laws of justice. Those who improve unclaimed lands, acquire
rights in them to the extent of the exchangable value

4

given them by their improvements. These rights are
bought and sold in all honest purchases and sales of
lands. Isral obtained Palestine by slaughtering and
enslaving its possessors, and plundered all their stores.
The land and its stores were no more given them, than
the booty of Bedouin Arabs, obtained by the murder
of its owners, is given them. Pirates and robbers
take their spoils in violation of divine laws, and acquire no just rights in them. It was so with the taking
of Palestine by Isral.

According to Gen. 17: 9—14, Shaddi enjoined circumcision early in the Abrahamic period, to be observed forever. The Hebrews abandoned sacrifices,
which were also to continue forever, after the destruction of Jerusalem in 70 A. D., but with the Moham-
medans, continue to practice circumcision. Jesus by
abandoning all these and other Jewish rites, signified
to all ages and nations, his rejection both of the Abrahamic covenants and Mosaic laws, and based his religion on laws universal and really divine, all of which
are included summarily, in justice, mercy, love, purity,
and truth.

No messengers from another planet are required to
bring us these laws, and no thunders from Sini to
proclaim them. We have them as perfectly by intu-
ition and reasoning from our experience and that of
others, as if they were brought by celestials from dis-
tant planets, or proclaimed by thunders from every
mountain and hill in the world. They underlie all
that is good and noble in human character, and the
contrary doings involve all that is possible of the evil
and odious.

According to Herodotus, circumcision began with the Egyptians or Ethiopians, and was received from them by several other nations. Sesostris third king of the twelfth dynasty, more than six hundred years before the beginning of the Abrahamic period, gave it to nations conquered by him. The Greeks were early acquainted with it, and held it in detestation. Among the Egyptians it was confined to the priests ; of the mummies, not one in fifty bears this mark.

The institution is based on the principle of marking animals by cropping the ear, and originated when men were without clothes and without shame ; it could not have originated later.

Jesus abandoned all ceremonies for right doings, and insisted on these alone. He put his disciples on the sole pursuit and practice of the good. But after his death, Peter, John and others imperfectly educated in his system, and bred from their childhood in that of the Pharisees, receded from his most advanced positions, preached Judaism entire, with Jesus as its Jeve in the flesh, till his death, had him resume the flesh on the third day, and ascend with it to heaven, a natural impossibility, and promised his return in a few years to complete the program of an earthly kingdom with Jerusalem for his capital, the Jews for his priests, and the whole world for his subjects.

Peter's experiment with this system was begun in A. D. 33 ; in 44, he went to Asia Minor and labored there about six years ; in 50, he went to Rome and founded the church there on a Judaic platform.

Paul entering the school of Jesus at Damascus a year or two after Peter began his departure from the scheme of Jesus at Jerusalem, persisted in rejecting circumcision ; but after some years admitted baptism, and instituted the Lord's Supper. Baptism with him was at first optional. In 58 A. D., when he had been twenty-three years in the field, he says in 1 Cor. 12 : 14, in regard to baptism, writing to a large church which he founded a few years before, I thank God, I baptized none of you but Crispus, Gaius and the house of Stephanas ; 17, For Christ sent me not to baptize, but to evangelize. According to this, converts were evangelized without being baptized, and baptism was an exceptional and not a general ordinance of Paul's Christionity at this time.

Paul, however, in 1 Cor. 15 : 29, refers to baptizing for the dead as a Christian rite, and in Rom. 6 : 3–61, has Christians buried with Christ by baptism into death, to walk in newness of life.

In the letter to the Galatians a few years before, baptism is not mentioned, and all that is required is walking in the spirit. Jesus required this and nothing more.

The Quakers, therefore, are right in rejecting all ceremonial institutions, as both anti-spiritual and anti-Christian. The little success of their movement, is owing to fatal mistakes connected with its truths, and to their rejecting a professional ministry. If there was a single story or two, or any number of stories to be rehearsed, as some imagine, or a few traditionary creeds to be kept along by church authority, a profes-sional ministry might be spared ; the books relating the stories and containing the creeds might suffice. But the church is a school of the highest learning and

culture, and is designed to aid men in fighting the
battles of life, against all perils. Every age has ne-
cessities never felt before. No books or lessons of the
past can ever meet all the needs of the present, and
sound religious faiths leave the old creeds far behind.
Theology is as progressive as the other sciences, and
its advances require to be continually received and
taught. God, the universe and men, have occupied
all past ages in their study and exposition, and will
occupy ages more. The pastor of a church has a task
in ministering to his charge, both in the public ser-
vices of the Sabbath and at other times, the demands
of which are not exceeded by those of any of the
learned professions. They require professional teach-
ers as much as colleges and universities. The design
of the churches is to elevate the toiling millions, and
give them at the least expense of time and money, the
means of the highest and best culture of their times.
To do this without a professional ministry is impossible; and the little success of the Quakers with the
exclusive possession of some of the most sublime positions ever taken by man, is an unanswerable argument
in favor of a professional ministry.

It seems strange to us that the Quakers do not per-
ceive their mistake in rejecting a professional ministry
and correct it. They are abundantly able to do it, and
with this and some other equally obvious corrections,
they would become directly one of the great powers of
the world.

Peter and Paul were heads of independent schools
of Christianity, and were mutually hostile, from 36 to
59 A. D., twenty-three years, when Paul accepted bap-

tism as an essential in place of circumcision, and Peter
abandoned the other Jewish rites. The two schools
from this time were consolidated, and took the name
of Catholics. No gospel was written till nearly a
hundred years after this arrangement, and those then
written conformed to the Catholic system as inaugu-
rated by Peter and Paul in 59 A. D.

The story of the baptism of Jesus by John, makes
no appearance in the New Testament letters. It first
appears near the middle of the second Christian century in the gospel according to Mark, and is copied
from it in the other gospels. The baptism, the prodigy
connected with it, and John's testimony to Jesus as
the Messiah, are all fictions of the second century, invented in conformity to a false theory of the Christian religion borrowed from the Pharisees. Jesus left
John entirely ; John upheld and intensified Judaism,
Jesus discarded it ; John mortified the body with severe fasting, as an enemy to be killed to save the soul ;
Jesus honored and cherished the body, and emancipa-
ted souls from vices and sins. John proclaimed the
kingdom of Jeve as predicted by Malachi, Daniel and
others, as at hand ; Jesus preached the reign of God
as universal and eternal. John's delusion has misled
many, and after prevailing 1800 years is surely pass-
ing away, while the truth declared by Jesus is on its
way to the conquest and redemption of the world, and
to the glory and rejoicing of the church.

Paul accepts Jesus as the Hebrew god Jeve in the
flesh, not the Supreme, but his son ; and has him set
aside the Jewish law as a work of angels, who framed
it with a sinister purpose to mislead men instead of

holding them always to the right and good. This is
signified by Gal. 3 : 19, 20. With this absurd theory
Paul fought Peter, Cephas and all who adhered to Judaism, twenty-three years, till he wrote his letter to
the Romans. In this he finds no fault with the Jewish law or its framers, but gets our release from it by
being baptized into the death of Jesus, through which
we are counted as having died with him and passed
beyond its jurisdiction, as all the dead have done.

Paul followed the mystic method of the other Pharisees of his time in giving the Abrhamic covenants
two senses, a natural sense, which was the only true
one, and a higher spiritual sense which was assumed
arbitrarily to support the equally false assumption of
their divine character. Jesus found no such sense in
the Abrahamic covenants, nor in any other of the Hebrew documents claimed as divine.

Paul in Gal. 3 : 1—4 : 10, has Jesus set aside the
Mosaic law, as a son of God and superior of the angels who ordered it and gave it by Jeve to Moses.
This is highly figurative, and proceeds on the assumption that Jesus by his death entered the spirit world
both of infernals and celestials, which he could not
enter otherwise.

In Gal. 3 : 19, Paul says, Why was the law given?
It was added to [the Abrhamic scheme] by hand of
a mediator [Jeve] ordered by angels, Charin for the
sake of the transgressions [of which it became the oc-
casion] till the seed came to whom the promise was
made.

The above is mistranslated in common versions. Paul's
assertion is that it was viciously to multiply transgres-

sions. Theodoret among the ancients, and Bloomfield
and other moderns make Moses this mediator, contrary
to the Pentateuch accounts on the subject, in which
the ordering angels never appear, and Jeve alone acts
for them. Where Paul finds his angels by whom the
law was ordered he does not say. Now according to
Paul, he acts against them, and in the person of Jesus
is exalted by the father to be a sovereign over them,
because they executed their trusts so badly.

Stephen is made to say in Acts 7 : 53, that the Hebrews received the law for ordinances on orders of
angels and did not keep it. This passage is obscure,
but its only consistent sense is that which we give
it, and this agrees with Gal. 3 : 19, where Paul
says the law was ordered by angels, and implies that
God had no hand in ordering it, because the mediator
Jeve represented many, and God is one.

In Gal. 4 : 1, 2, Paul makes subjection to the Jewish law, that of an heir during his minority to guar-
dians and stewards ; and in verses 4 and 5, has the
god send his son when we came to be of age, and redeem us from the Stoicheia, constellations, the twelve
signs of Zodiac, that we may be sons of God, and not
of the constellations. Paul here identifies the twelve
constellations of the Zodiac with the angels that ordered the Jewish law, and has Jesus redeem us from
them.

This argument is abstruse and has been accepted as
profound on the credit of its author, by thousands that
understood no part of it but the conclusion against the
Jewish law. It misrepresents the constellations, the
Christian religion, and the dealings of God with men.

All men are sons of God by creation and never had any other master. The constellations are as far from having ordered the Jewish law as the Alps and Andes or the Rocky Mountains of North America.

3. *History and Chronology of the Hebrews in their Pa-triarchal period.*

The period represented by the patriarchs begins with the migration of the Hebrews from Syria, and represents them by Abram, who migrates from Syria to Palestine at the age of seventy-five, and sojourns there a hundred years, when he is succeeded by Isaac at seventy-five, who sojourns there a hundred and five years. Jacob and Esau are born when their father is sixty, Gen. 25 : 26, and Jacob succeeds to the pa-triarchate in Palestine at a hundred and twenty, at his father's death ; Esau founds and rules the kindred nation of the Edomites.

Before this Jacob goes back to Syria ; after seven years in that country marries two sisters, and in the next thirteen years, Gen. 31 : 88, has eleven sons and one daughter by his wives and their two maid ser-vants. The last son born in Syria was Joseph, Gen. 30 : 24. Joseph is thirty years old when he stands before Pharoe, Gen. 41 : 46 ; and Jacob at a hun-dred and thirty goes down to Egypt, in the second year of the famine, when Joseph is thirty-nine, Gen. 45 : 11.

According to this, Joséph was born when his father was ninety-one, and all the eleven sons were born when he was between seventy-eight and ninety-one. It fol-lows that Jacob's flight to Syria twenty years before

he left it, was at the age of seventy-two, when his
father was a hundred and thirty-two, and at his return to Palestine after an absence of twenty years, he
and Esau his twin brother, were ninety-two.

This chronology is too extravagant for history ; but
it is continuous, making two hundred and fifteen years
from the migration of Abraham from Syria to Pales-
estine to that of Jacob from Palestine to Egypt. Jacob sojourns seventeen years in Egypt, and is succeeded by Levi his third son by Leah, born appa-
rently in the third year after his marriage, when his
father was eighty-one, which makes him sixty-six at
his father's death, and gives him a patriarchate of
seventy-one years, leaving a hundred and twenty-
two years to be divided between Kohath and Amram·
We divide this equally, giving them sixty-one years
each. Kohath dies at a hundred and thirty-three,
and Amram at one hundred thirty-seven.

Amram makes no appearance at the founding of
theocracy, and his death was probably the occasion of
the recall of Moses to Egypt, when a successor was to
be appointed. Aaron was entitled to succeed his father
from priority of birth, but Moses was the ablest and
most experienced in civil and military affairs, and
takes precedence of his older brother. But instead of
following in the track of the previous chiefs, Moses
changes the government to a theocracy, in which he
serves as judge, and Aaron as priest.

The author of the history of the exode tells us in
Ex. 12 : 40, that the sojourning of the sons of Isral
in Egypt was four hundred and thirty years, which
following the method of Josephus in his antiquities of

the Jews, in 93 A. D., interpreters explain as taking
us back to the migration of Abram and including the
Palestinian period. On the contrary, the author of
this notice ignores the accounts of the sojourning of
Abraham, Isaac and Jacob in Palestine, doubtless
aware of their fictitious character. The sons of Isral
went down to Egypt and sojourned there when their
reputed father was a hundred and thirty years old,
and the time of their sojourning there, according to
Ex. 12 : 40, was four hundred and thirty years.
Having misled both Jews and Christians by reducing
the Egyptian period of the Hebrews from four hundred
and thirty years to two 'hundred and fifteen in his
antiquities of the Jews, in his work against Apion,
written seven years later in 100 A. D., when he was
sixty-three, he gives an account of that period from
Manetho, making it much longer. His findings as
reported in his last work are as follows :

In Apion 1 : 14, he says, Manetho was by birth an
Egyptian, but made himself master of Greek learning.
He wrote the history of his country in Greek, trans-
lating it from their sacred records.

In his second book he writes concerning us as follows : I will set down his very words, as if to bring
him into court, for a witness.

We had a king whose name was Timaus [the last
king of the 14th dynasty]; under him God was
against us, and it came to pass, I know not how, that
men of ignoble birth from the east, made an expedition into our country, and became masters of it without our hazarding a battle.

When they had our rulers in their power, they

burned our cities, demolished the temples of the gods,
killed some and enslaved some. At length they made
one of themselves, whose name was Salatis, king. He
lived at Memphis, put Upper and Lower Egypt under
tribute and established garrisons at suitable places.
He aimed chiefly to protect the eastern districts, fore-
seeing that the Assyrians who were then dominant,
would attack them. Finding in the Saite Nome a city
on the Bubastic channel called Avaris, [Hebrais], he
rebuilt it, put strong walls round it, and put in it a
garrison of 240,000 men.

Salatis came there in the summer to gather his grain,
pay and train his soldiers, and impress foreigners with
fear.

The dynasty founded by this king is the 15th ; it
is reported by Josephus and Africanus.

| By Josephus. | | By Africanus. | |
Kings,	Years, m.		
1. Salatis,..........	13	Saitis,...........	19
2. Beon,...........	44	Benon, ...	44
3. Apachnas,.......	36–7	Pachnan,.........	61
4. Apophis,........	61	Staan,...........	50
5. Ionias, ...	50–1	Archles,..........	49
6. Assis,...........	49–2	Aphobis, ...	1
Total,........	253–10		284

These six were the first rulers among them, and this
whole nation was called Hycsos [Hebrews], that is
shepherd kings ; for Hyc signifies king in the sacred
dialect, and Sos shepherd in the common dialect ; but
some say that they were Arabs.

These people whom we have called kings and shepherds, and their descendants, ruled Egypt, [the 16th
dynasty], 511 years.

After this [under the 17th dynasty of 151 years],
the kings of Thebais and other parts of Egypt made
an insurrection against them, and there was a terrible
and long war. [Still later], the shepherds were van-
quished and driven out of the rest of Egypt by Alis-
phragmuthoris [sixth king of the 18th dynasty], and
shut up in a place called Avaris [Hebrais], containing
10,000 acres, which they fortified and defended,
[Alisphragmuthosis dying] Thummosis [called by
Africanus, Touthmosis], endeavored to take the shepherds by assault and siege with 480,000 men ; but
failing in this, the Egyptians agreed that they should
leave Egypt and seek homes elsewhere, when [in 1640
B. C.] not less than 240,000 foot left with their
families and effects, going through the wilderness to
Syria ; but from fear of the Assyrians, they built a
city in the country now called Judea, large enough to
accommodate this great number of men, and called it
Jerusalem.

After further reporting the kings of the 18th dynasty and finding Danaus under its last king, Josephus says in Apion 1 : 16 : "This is Manetho's account,
and it is evident that these shepherds, who were no
other than our forefathers, were delivered from Egypt
393 years [the time he finds for the 18th dynasty]
before Danaus came to Argos, and almost 1000 years
before the siege of Troy."

Josephus here confounds the exode with the fall of
the 17th dynasty, while he had just before reported it

from Manetho as occurring under Thummosis, the son
and successor of Misphragmuthoris, seventh king of
the 18th dynasty.

The oppression began at the fall of the 17th dynasty, but the exode was under the seventh king of the
18th dynasty.

Julius Africanus bishop of Nicopolis in Palestine at
about 225 A. D. reports the Egyptian period of the
Hebrews here described by Josephus as follows : 15th
dynasty of Hycsos, as we have stated, six kings 284
years ; 16th, thirty kings 518 years ; 17th, forty-three
kings 151 years ; total, 953 years; the oppression under seven kings of the 18th dynasty, 124 years ; grand
total of the Egyptian period, 1077 years.

These notices show clearly that the Hebrew accounts
are not historic. Abraham, Isaac and Jacob correspond obscurely to the 15th, 16th and 17th dynasties
of the Hebrews in Egypt, not in Palestine, and are
delineated as model men. Abraham is model man I.,
the man of faith ; Isaac is model man II., the dutiful
son, and man of peace ; and Jacob is model man III.,
the man of craft, in strong contrast with his twin
brother, the father of the Edomites, whose simplicity
is a warning against a like fault. The removal of
these model men from Egypt to Palestine, is a grave
fault in the stories considered as historic fictions. It
was designed, however, to help the claim to have been
promised the land by their gods, in those early periods,
a help that was much needed to give them currency.

The first seven kings of the 18th dynasty.

		B. C.	Years.
1.	Amosis,	1764	25
2.	Chebros,	1739	13
3.	Amenophthis,	1726	24
4.	Amersis,	1702	22
5.	Misaphris,	1680	13
6.	Misphragsmuthosis,	1667	26
7.	Touthmasis,	1641	9

Exode in 1640 *B. C.*

We find this date of the exode as follows: Moses ruled the nation 40 years, Joshua 25, the judges after Joshua supplying 30 years for Samuel, 480, Saul and David 80, and Solomon founded the house of Jeve in the fourth year of his reign, which is 1012 B. C. This is the first certain date after the exode. Going back from 1012 B. C., we have the founding of the monarchy under Saul in 1095 B. C., the death of Joshua in 1575, and the exode in 1640.

We harmonize Manetho with these computations by advancing the founding of the 18th dynasty to 1764 B. C.; from the exode in 1640 B. C., and we go back according to Manetho 1077 years, to 2717 B. C., for the migration of the Hebrews from Syria to Egypt and the founding of the first dynasty there.

We deem the Hebrew estimate of the time of their exode reliable, because it is the date of the founding of the theocracy, because they received letters and began to commit their traditions to writing before the fall of the theocracy in 1095 B. C., and because they give us the intervening periods in specific sums, if we accept twenty-five years from Josephus for Joshua, and supply thirty for Samuel.

Had no information reached us concerning their Egyptian period except that of the Hebrew sacred books, their enigmas would have no key for their solution ; the information furnished by Manetho makes them intelligible.

The Egyptians called the Hebrews Hycsos, interpreted to signify shepherd kings. Hycsos differs no more from Hebrews than Sesonchis from Shishak, the Hebrew name by which he was called. The Hebrews are as clearly meant by the Hycsos of Manetho as if he had called them Hebrews.

Josephus was a learned Pharisee of the priestly caste. It was a common error of the Pharisees to magnify their own national books unreasonably and disparage the works of other nations. The acknowledgement of Josephus that Manetho described the Hebrews correctly in the passages above quoted, shows an extraordinary triumph of truth over bigotry and superstition.

Prudential considerations led him to ignore the discrepancies between the Egyptian and Hebrew accounts, and as far as possible to conceal them. This appears from the brevity and obscurity of his references to the 16th and 17th dynasties, while he reports the 15th and 18th in full.

The inconsideration with which these findings of Josephus have been set aside by Christian critics, is not creditable to their scholarship. Sound and thorough scholarship is of modern date and has grown out

of the superior advantages and culture of modern
times.

Menes, according to Manetho. founds his thirty dynasties in 5799 B. C., long before the Hebrew epoch
of creation, and reigns sixty-two years. We ascertain
this date by tracing the numbers of Manetho back
from 1640, the time of the exode, first to 1764 B. C.,
the year in which the 18th dynasty was founded, as
shown by the Hebrew date of the exode, and thence
through the seventeen earlier dynasties to the first.
There is room for errors here as in series III., and
Menes may have reigned a hundred years earlier
than this. Errors are more likely to occur by omis-
sion than by addition or repetition, though they are
possible in all these ways, and in others.

It appears from Manetho that the Hebrews had
their own government and military organization under
the 18th dynasty. According to the Hebrew books,
they were a single people till they were divided into
tribes by the sons of Jacob, eleven of whom became
heads of single tribes, bearing their names, while Joseph by his two sons, Manasse and Aphrim, founded
two tribes. At the close of their Egyptian period,
twelve of these tribes were of the military and shepherd caste, and one, that of Levi, neither acted as soldiers nor shepherds, but found employment as priests
with the twelve military tribes, whence their dispersion, as noticed in Ex. 49: 7. The tribe of Simeon
may at an earlier period have been of a similar caste,
and had a similar dispersion ; but on leaving Egypt
they are numbered with the military and shepherd
tribes.

5

Let none deem it a matter of indifference whether
the facts are made to appear in this portion of sacred
history, or the old impositions and mistakes are kept
along unquestioned. Delusions are like the breaking
out of waters, when they fill their channels, and are
prepared to sweep every thing away with them, or
like the kindling of forest fires, that small at first,
may be extinguished with a breath, but directly gain
a force and fury as they proceed that laugh to scorn
the efforts of thousands to arrest them. These accounts
begin a breach that has deluged the world, and have
kindled fires that rage uncontrolled and uncontrollable
through all later times. We find a mighty river of
delusions overflowing and devastating Christendom
with waters of death; we go to its fountain and by
correcting that, convert it into the river of the waters
of life eternal.

Secular scientists are all agreed throughout the
world, none gainsay or distrust the findings of their
fellows. Why is this reversed in the religious field?
Religious science is in no way different from secular;
one law governs both. The mischief with religious
science begins small and subtle with the impositions
and misjudgments of the early Hebrews, in which the
boldest, and in some cases the most absurd fictions are
accepted for facts. These begin small, but grow large
as they proceed and give rise to divisions and con-
flicting sects innumerable. First we have Jews and
Christians; then Christians divide as Catholics, Ori-
ental churches, the Greek church and the Protestants.
Then Protestants divide endlessly; and many of those
divisions and subdivisions are mutually hostile, while

another class of thinkers denounce all religious sciences so called, as delusions or infected with fatal
errors. All this conflict of opinions begins with the
frauds and fictions of the early Hebrews; and from
this one fountain come forth many streams of turbid
and unwholesome waters. The world has long tried
to correct and purify the streams in vain, without dis-
turbing their fountain. We propose to purify the
fountain, and leave the streams to take from it only
pure and healthful waters. This remedy is possible
and effectual; no other is. It must be accepted; it
must be applied; its benefits will be infinite; it will
give us a regenerated world.

4. *History and Chronology of the Egyptians, according to Manetho, in 280 B. C., as reported by Julius
Africanus in 230 A. D.*

We introduce this in corroboration of what precedes.

The older families of the Caucasians are the Chaldeans, Hebrews, Arabs, Syrians and Egyptians. After
these follow the Celts, Teutons, Greeks, Latins, Hin-
dus, Medes, Persians, Tartars, Russians, Georgians,
Circasians, Turks, etc.

The great historian of Egypt was Manetho. He
lived under the first two Ptolemies, Greek kings of
Egypt, from 300 to 247 B. C., directly after the times
of Alexander the Great, of whom the elder Ptolemy
and founder of the Egyptian dynasty was a half brother, being a son of Philip.

Manetho belonged to the priestly caste of Egypt,
was versed in all its occult sciences, and was master of
the Greek language and literature at a time when Al-

exandria rivaled Athens as a seat of the best Greek culture, and when the Greek kings of Syria and Egypt were the lights of the world.

Manetho wrote the history of his country in Greek for the information of the Greek literati, translating much of it from contemporary annals and other documents that were never before reported to the world, and have since perished. His work early disappears, but not till Josephus in 100 A. D., copied portions of it relating to the Hebrews, called by the Egyptians Hycsos ; and Julius Africanus, generally known as Africanus the African, a Christian bishop of Nicopolis in Palestine, at about 230 A. D., copied his prehistoric periods to Menes, and thirty dynasties from Menes to the death of Nectanebus II., in 339 B. C., seven years before Egypt submitted to Alexander the Great.

Africanus called his work Annals of the World, in five books. It was highly esteemed by the ancients, and portions of it were often copied. They have lost none of their importance by the unprecedented progress of all the sciences history included, in our times; but have rather gained.

Africanus incorporated an abstract of the work of Manetho in his annals, supposing, however, that Manetho's earlier periods were too much prolonged; though not doubting that he reported what he found. He accepted the Septuagint date of creation as historic, computed to be in 5799 B. C.

Eusebius, bishop of Cæsarea and moderator of the famous Council of Nice in 324 A. D., under Constantine, besides writing a history of the church, copied

the annals of Africanus at about 330 A. D., both of
which are still preserved, and held in great respect.

The work of Eusebius was copied by George, a
monk of Constantinople called Syncellus, as occupying
a cell with the bishop. Syncellus began his work in
792 A. D., at the Septuagint epoch of creation, which
he computed to be 5500 B. C., and continued it to the
reign of Maximin, when he died, leaving the work un-
finished.

Manetho, as we compute the times of his dynasties,
begins them in 5799 B. C., 300 years before the Septuagint epoch of creation, and finds still longer periods
before Menes than after him.

No intelligent critic doubts that in these prehistoric
periods, Manetho reports what he found, and judged
to be reliable. He had with scholars of his age, and
of centuries that followed, the highest credit for scholarship, honesty and veracity. But his numbers in
dealing with the earliest times, were deemed too large
to be credible, and were generally dismissed with little
consideration. Modern discovery has in our day come
wonderfully to his aid.

Animals do not count; a counting animal would be
a prodigy. Counting was invented by men, first to
the number of 10, that of the fingers and thumbs of
the two hands. Then came adding and multiplying
to hundreds, and from hundreds to thousands, all of
which are multiples 10.

Years were early noted and counted, and time was
naturally estimated in years and generations. Counting by hundreds and thousands was reached long before the other arts were perfected that appear under

Menes and his successors; and the advance of our Caucasian fathers from the counting stage to that of the higher arts, may have been very slow.

As soon as years were observed they would be counted by tens, hundreds and thousands. Counts could be recorded by points and lines, as soon as they were reached, and they only required to be made continuous to measure the longest periods.

If men existed in Egypt with the art of counting, and the knowledge of years, in 30,000 B. C., and with the higher arts of brick making and pottery, the years from that time may have all been counted, and the counts kept along by the priests, kings and other chiefs of those early ages. It is conceded by all competent judges that Egyptian civilization did not begin with Menes or his immediate predecessors, but came down from much earlier periods.

PART I.

Prehistoric Periods.

1. The reign of gods beginning with the god of fire, and ending with god Horus; time indefinite.

	B. C.	Years.
2. Other gods to Bytis	30,725	13,900
3. Gods and heroes	16,825	1,255
Names not preserved.		
4. Human kings	15,570	1,817
5. Thirty kings of Memphis	13,753	1,790
6. Ten kings of This	11,963	350
7. Gosts and heroes	11,613	5,813
End of series	5,800	Total, 24,925

Not a solitary name of any inventor, discoverer or king is reported from this long period. Several of its gods, however, are reported by name, because they were kept along in following periods.

In 1851 Abbas Pasha began to interrogate the Nile valley as to the age of its occupancy, by digging and examining works imbedded in its constantly rising soil ; and after his death his explorations were contin- ued by his successor to 1854.

They employed several able engineers and sixty workmen during the times when the river was lowest, and dug twenty-seven pits in the parallel of Memphis in a line extending across the valley, and fifty-one eight miles above the apex of the Delta.

When they reached water they resorted to borings and went still further down. They found the bottom of the alluvium on the edges of the valley, but in the central parts it was in no case reached.

In the portions explored, they found many human and animal remains, but no remains of animals that became extinct before man appeared. In some places the diggings were extensive for the first sixteen or twenty feet down, and jars, vases, pots, a small hu- man figure of burnt clay, a copper knife, and other articles of human manufacture were found.

If the average rise of the alluvium was six inches in a century, in the part penetrated by one of the bor- ings, burnt brick found at the depth of sixty feet were 12,000 years old. A fragment was found at a depth of seventy-two feet near the apex of the Delta, two or three feet below the surface of the Mediterra- nean, where the deposits are estimated at two and half

inches in a century, which makes the finding 30,000
years old.

A depth of 20,000 or 30,000 years was explored,
but the period preceding man's works was not reached·

The ablest geologists in Europe took great interest
in these explorations, and the results agree with their
findings elsewhere, both before and since, in caves
that were gradually filled on the margins of rivers
and seas, carrying back the age of man to a much
more remote past than is reported by Manetho.

Christianity has no interest in defending the Hebrew estimates of the age of the earth made under the
Davidic kings, against her own testimonies. God's
works speak for themselves, and refuse to be dwarfed
or to have their periods greatly abridged.

It is no just disparagement of religion that ages and
generations were required to disengage it from vicious
prejudices and errors. All science, religious and secular, is built up like the earth itself, terrace by terrace, each terrace above its ocean levels, being the
work of long ages.

The advance of knowledge has both occupied long
periods and been attended with long pauses, diver-
sions and retrogressions; but the force behind both
the earth and the sciences is never exhausted nor over-
come. It is only arrested for relatively short periods,
to be a final victor after all possible defeats; and is
thenceforward forever undisputed and indisputable,
an infallible divine law for human guidance, and an
unfailing ministry to human good.

Menes in Egyptian history, follows uncounted generations of Caucasians.

4. Thirty dynasties in three series.
SERIES I.

FOURTEEN EARLY DYNASTIES BEGINNING WITH MENES.

Dynasties	Kings.	B. C.	Years.	Capitals.
1	8	5799	263	This.
2	9	5536	302	"
3	9	5234	214	Memphis.
4	8	5020	284	"
5	8	4736	218	Elephantine.
6	6	4518	203	Memphis.
7	70	4315	706	"
8	28	4315	146	"
9	19	4169	409	Heracleopolis.
10	19	3760	185	"
11	17	3575	59	Diospolis.
12	7	3516	160	"
13	60	3356	453	"
14	70	2903	184	Xoite.
End of series,	2719		3078	

The kings of Series I. were largely engaged in building. They also carried on many predatory wars, took numerous domestic animals, and many captives whom they held as slaves and employed on their works. Pyramid building ended with them. Many pyramids have disappeared. On the west bank of the Nile sixty-nine remain in groups through a distance of sixty miles. The largest, that of Cheops [Keops], stands on about thirteen acres for its base, and is 480 feet high. Next to the pyramids in importance are obelisks, sphinxes, palaces, statues colossal and life sizes, temples and tombs. The sphinxes are of both sexes, mostly males to represent kings, the females represent queens.

SERIES II.

15TH, 16TH AND 17TH DYNASTIES, THE HYCSOS, SHEPHERD
KINGS OR HEBREWS.

Dynasties	Kings.	B. C.	Years.	Capitals.
15	6	2618	284	Memphis.
16	30	2434	518	"
17	43	1917	151	"
End of series,		1765	953	

The Hebrews did no building and no permanent
structures were erected in their times. They main-
tained an expensive standing army, but seem to have
had no foreign wars. They invaded the country from
Arabia and were the superiors of the Egyptians in the
arts of war and the care of domestic animals.

SERIES III.

THIRTEEN LATER DYNASTIES, BEGINNING WITH THE 18TH.

Dynasties	Kings.	B. C.	Reigns.	Capitals.
18	16	1666	287	Diospolis.
19	6	1379	204	"
20	12	1175	135	"
21	7	1040	114	Tanis.
22	9	926	116	Bubastis.
23	4	810	89	Tanis.
24	1	721	6	Sais.
25	3	715	40	Ethiopia.
26	9	675	150	Sais.
27	8	525	122	Persia.
28	1	403	6	Native.
29	4	397	20	"
30	3	377	38	"
End of series,		339	1327	

Series III. opens with the most illustrious of all the dynasties, from which we infer that the Egyptians profited by their Hebrew masters. Their old time arts are instantly revived and shine forth in their temples, obelisks, palaces, statues and tombs with a glory never exceeded before nor since. Pyramid build-ing ceased before the Hycsos invasion, never to be re-vived.

EIGHTEENTH DYNASTY, DISPOLIS.

	B. C.	Corrected.	Yrs.
1. Amosis	1666	1764	25
2. Chebros...................	1641	1739	13
3. Amenophthis..............	1628	1726	24
4. Amerses..................	1604	1702	22
5. Misaphris...............	1582	1680	13
6. Misphragmuthosis..	1569	1667	26
7. Touthmosis	1543	1641	9
Exode.....................	—	1640	—
8. Amenophis................	1534	1632	31
9. Horus....................	1503	1601	37
10. Acherres.................	1466	1564	32
11. Rathos	1434	1534	6
12. Chebres.................	1438	1526	12
13. Acherres.................	1416	1514	12
14. Armesses	1404	1503	5
15. Ramesses................	1399	1497	1
16. Amenopath...............	1398	1496	19
	1399	1477	287

This correction is made from the Hebrew date of the exode, by accepting from Josephus 25 years for Joshua as judge, and supplying 30 for Samuel. Count-ing back from the founding of the house of Jeve in the fourth year of Solomon, which was 1012 B. C., we find the founding of the monarchy under Saul in

1095, the death of Joshua 480 years before, in 1575 B. C., put by mistake in 1 Kings 6 : 1, for the period from the exode to the founding of the house of Jeve, the exode in 1640, and the founding of the 18th dynasty in 1764 B. C.

Other dates of the founding of the 18th dynasty are as follows : By Eusebius, bishop of Cæsarea, under Constantine, 330 A. D., as computed from the Latin text of Jerome 1798 B. C., as computed from the Armenian text 1792 B. C. According to the old chronicle for the 19th, 20th and 21st dynasties, supplemented by the numbers of Africanus for the 18th, 1801. Bunsen finds the founding of the 18th dynasty in 1625 B. C. and the exode in 1540 ; Dr. Hales finds the exode in 1648, a much nearer approximation to the truth than 1491, generally accepted, to the shame of Christendom. Josephus and Eusebius find the Greek Egyptus and Danaus at the close of the 18th dynasty under the names of Sethoris and Armais.

The 18th and sixth are the most extraordinary of all the dynasties, though several produced great conquerors.

TWENTY-SECOND DYNASTY, BUBASTIS.

		Corrected.	
1. Sesonchis [Shishak]	927	980	21
2. Osorthon	906	959	15
3–5. Three kings, not named.....	891	944	25
6. Tacellothis................	866	919	13
7–9. Three kings, not named.....	853	906	42
	811	864	116

Shishak appears in 1 Kings 11 : 40, proximately

in 980 B. C., as giving Jeroboam an asylum in Egypt, when he fled from Isral on account of conspiring against Solomon to divide his kingdom. He appears again in 1 Kings 14 : 25, 26, as taking and plundering Jerusalem in the fifth year of Rehoboam, which was 971 B. C. Assuming that 980 was the first year of his reign, his taking of Jerusalem was in his ninth year. Our correction carries back the dates of this dynasty 53 years to allow this.

TWENTY-SIXTH DYNASTY, SAIS.

			Corrected.
1. Stephinates	676	7	686
2. Nechepsos	669	6	679
3. Necho I.	663	8	673
4. Psammitichus....	655	54	665
5. Necho II.................	601	6	611
6. Psammuthis II.	595	6	605
7. Uaphris....	589	19	599
8. Amosis II.................	570	44	580
9. Psammecherites	526	6 m	536
		150½	

According to 2 Kings 23 : 29, Necho II. invaded Assyria, and while on this expedition killed king Josiah at Megiddo in 610 B. C. According to Africanus he began to reign in 601, nine years after this, and reigned six years. If his invasion of Assyria was in the second year of his reign, these dates should be put back ten years, and we so correct them.

Inquirers need not marvel at these shortcomings of numbers. In dealing with numbers, omissions are easy and almost inevitable, and the just presumption is, that in these cases the errors occurred by omissions made inadvertently, or from defective copies. By substituting the larger numbers of Eusebius in certain cases for those of Africanus, we get all the extension of time required ; but the method we have finally adopted is to correct Africanus in the dynasties in which he is certainly wrong, and leave his numbers elsewhere unchanged.

Cambyses reigned over Persia $6\frac{5}{12}$ years, that is a part of seven years, and conquered Egypt in the fifth year of his reign. This allows him three years over Egypt, only by counting the fifth and part of the seventh as full years. Cambyses met with heavy losses in Egypt, and revenged them on the Egyptians with great severity and cruelty. His hostility to the priests knew no bounds, and he stripped the temples of their wealth. After becoming embittered to the point of madness against the Egyptians, he exercised cruelties against his Persian subjects, which can be accounted for only on the supposition of lunacy. This is favored by the fact that he was an epileptic, retaining, however, his great abilities. Providentially, he died by an accidental wound inflicted by his own sword early in life.

Nectanebus II., the third and last king of the 30th dynasty at Sebennys, was driven out of Egypt after a disturbed reign of eighteen years, by an aspirant to the throne from Mendes, whose name is not preserved, and took refuge in Ethiopia. Better generalship might have saved his dynasty seven years longer, till in 332 submission to Alexander became a military necessity.

The Egyptians had fallen far behind the Greeks in intellectual, moral and physical culture, and in 332

B. C., effectual resistance to Alexander was impossible. Alexander found Egypt again subject to Persia, and was accepted as a deliverer rather than a conqueror. While he lived, the country was ruled under him by Ptolemy Lagus, his half brother, one of his ablest generals. After Alexander's death in 323 B. C., Ptolemy founded the dynasty of the Ptolemies in Egypt, which continued 300 years, when in 30 B. C. Egypt became a province of the Roman empire.

Egypt was conquered by the Caliph Omer in 640, by the Turks in 1517, by France near the close of the 18th century, and in 1801 was restored to Turkey by England. In 1811 it became independent under Mehemet Ali, but is now again a dependency of Turkey, and the kedive, its ruler, pays the imperial government at Constantinople $700,000 a year, and has the power of making treaties and having armies. The nation is heavily in debt, and the people are in great poverty and misery. The present population is 2,800,000, chiefly Copts, Fellahs, Arabs and Turks. The Turks bear rule. The Copts are the descendants of the higher classes of the ancient Egyptians, and the Fellahs of the laborers. The Coptic and Abyssinian churches do little for the elevation of their peoples.

History is chiefly valuable for its lessons of the practical working of the divine laws. These lessons are yet but partially mastered.

www.ingramcontent.com/pod-product-compliance
Lightning Source LLC
Chambersburg PA
CBHW020326090426
42735CB00009B/1428